Storms

Miriam Busch Goin

NATIONAL GEOGRAPHIC
Washington, D.C.

To S.R. and N.J. — forces of nature, both. — M.B.G.

Library of Congress Cataloging-in-Publication Data
Goin, Miriam.
Storms! / by Miriam Goin.
p. cm.
ISBN 978-1-4263-0394-4 (pbk. : alk. paper) -- ISBN 978-1-4263-0395-1 (lib. bdg. : alk. paper)
1. Storms--Juvenile literature. I. Title.
QC941.3.G65 2009
551.55--dc22
2008051883

COVER, 26-27 bottom: © Visuals Unlimited/ Corbis; 1: © Pekka Parviainen/ Photo Researchers, Inc.; 2:
© David Epperson/ Stone/ Getty Images; 4: © Roy Corral/ Stone/ Getty Images; 4-5: © Phil Degginger/ Alamy;
5: © Danny Lehman/ Corbis; 6-7, 32 top left: © Roine Magnusson/ Stone/ Getty Images; 8-9, 32 bottom left:
© Jhaz Photography/ Shutterstock; 10 left, 10-11, 14-15, 32 bottom right: © Gene Rhoden/ Weatherpix Stock Images;
12 top: © IntraClique/ Shutterstock; 12-13: © Sebastian Knight/ Shutterstock; 13 right: © Warren E. Faidley/DRK Photo;
16-17: © Ingo Arndt/ Minden Pictures/ NationalGeographicStock.com; 18-19: © Hiroyuki Matsumoto/ Photographer's
Choice/ Getty Images; 20-21: © Steve McCurry/ NationalGeographicStock.com; 22-23: © Mike Hill/ Alamy; 24-25: © NASA/
JPL/SSI; 26-27 top: © Anatoli Styf/ Shutterstock; 27 top: © Kazuyoshi Nomachi/ Corbis; 27 bottom, 32 top right: © Solvin
Zankl/ Photographer's Choice/ Getty Images; 28: © JTB Photo Communications, Inc./ Alamy; 29 top: © Alvaro Leiva/
Photolibrary.com; 29 bottom: © Science Faction/ Getty Images; 30: © Norbert Rosing/ National Geographic/
Getty Images; 31 top: © Gustavo Fadel/ Shutterstock; 31 bottom: © Jaipal Singh/ epa/ Corbis.

National Geographic supports K-12 educators with
ELA COMMON CORE RESOURCES.
Visit www.natgeoed.org/commoncore

Printed in China
Storms: 14/PPS/6 Weather: 14/PPS/3 Rocks & Minerals: 14/PPS/3 Volcanoes: 14/PPS/9

Table of Contents

Weather!

Storms are important.
Living things need fresh water
from rain and snow.

Wind can help clean the air.
Weather cools and heats our
planet so it is just right for life.

Clouds are made of drops of water so small they float.

These clouds look heavy and gray. Can you hear the wind blow? Leaves wave back and forth on branches. What's happening? Wild, wonderful, stormy weather!

Weather Words

Weather:
What it is
like outside.

Thunder and Lightning

Flash! Boom!

In these storm clouds, the drops of water have frozen. Little ice crystals are bumping wildly against big crystals. This makes lightning. Lightning heats the air quickly. This very fast temperature change makes sound waves. The sound is thunder!

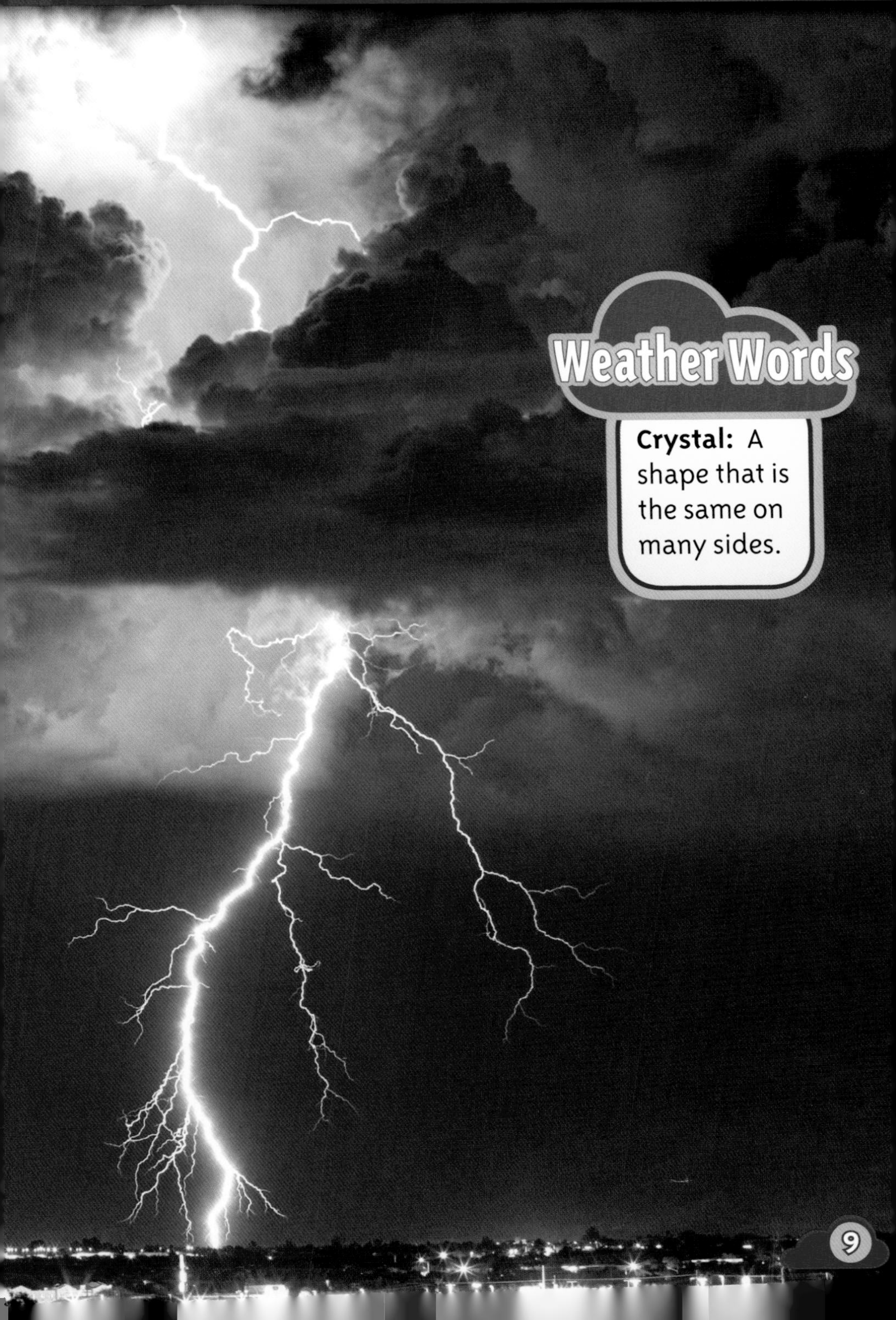

Weather Words

Crystal: A shape that is the same on many sides.

Lightning is electricity.
It is hotter than the sun.
Some lightning jumps from
cloud to cloud. Some jumps from
the ground to the sky.

Lightning can make loops and
patterns in the sky. It can even roll
in a ball. Lightning bolts can travel
sixty miles or more.

Q What did one lightning bolt say to the other?

A You are shocking.

Weather Words

Electricity: Energy that can be natural or man-made.

This is ribbon lightning. It happens when strong winds push the lightning bolts sideways.

11

Hailstorm

Thunk! Clunk!
Some thunderstorms make
hailstones. Hailstones are not
stones. They are ice.

Ice crystals in some thunderclouds get tumbled in the cloud. They get bigger and bigger until they are so heavy they fall. Hail can be big or small. It can be round or long.

An unusually big hailstone!

Tornado

Strong winds blow.
Dark clouds cover the sky.
Hail falls. Suddenly, it is quiet.
In the distance, a cone-shaped
funnel cloud touches the ground.
Tornado! Twister! Cyclone!
These are all names for a fierce,
fast, twisting wind.

Over water, tornadoes are called
"waterspouts."

Weather Words

Funnel:
A cone shape, wider at the top.

Sandstorm

A wall of wind picks up sand.
As the wind crosses the land,
it picks up more sand. The
wall grows higher.

When it roars past, it can knock down fences. In Australia they call the storms willy-willys. In Sudan, they call them haboobs.

Blizzard

Snowflakes fall from very cold clouds. A cold wind blows the snow so hard you cannot see in front of you.

Snowflakes are ice crystals. In a blizzard there are billions and trillions of snowflakes.

Monsoon

Monsoons are winds that change each season. India has only two seasons. Winter monsoons are dry.

Summer monsoons bring LOTS
of rain. Everyone cheers because
the rains help food grow

Hurricane

It is late summer. Dark clouds form over the ocean. Strong winds pull ocean water up into spinning clouds. Hurricane! Cyclone! Typhoon! Hurricane winds knock down houses. Water floods streets and homes. Hurricane winds spin in a circle. The middle of a hurricane is still and calm. It is called the "eye" of the storm.

Out of this World!

Where are the worst storms?
Not on Earth!

Jupiter's hurricane has been blowing for more than 400 years! In 2006 a lightning storm on Saturn lasted for weeks. The lightning bolts were more than 1,000 times stronger than Earth's! Neptune has winds that blow 900 miles per hour!

Jupiter's hurricane is called the Great Red Spot.

Guess!

Storms are made of many
small parts. Together with wind,
these tiny bits are strong!
Guess what each tiny bit is.

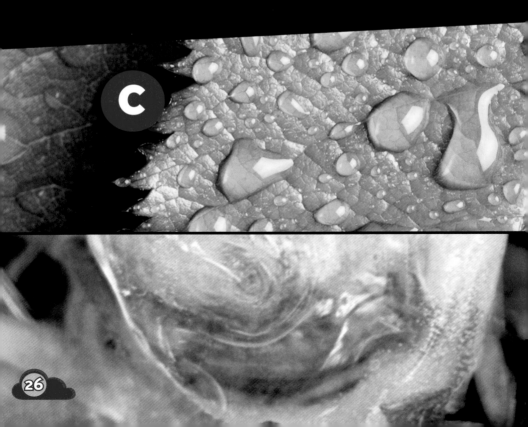

C

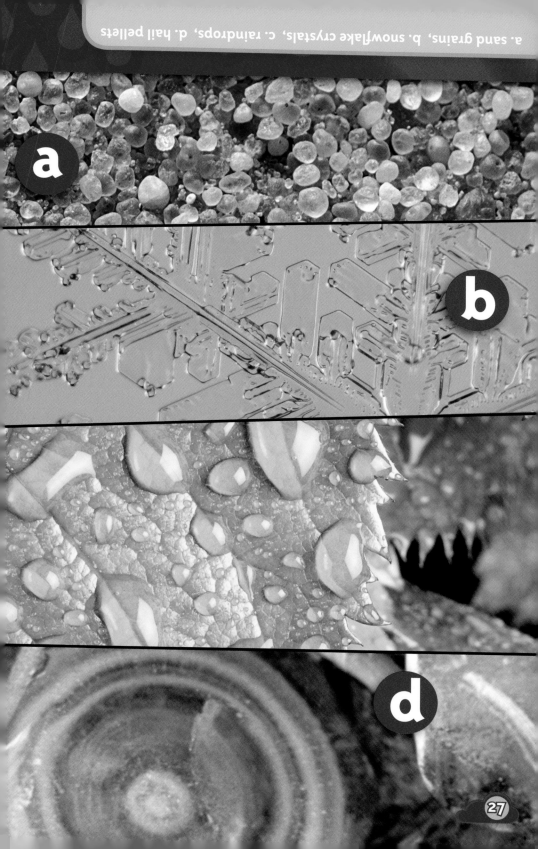

House for a Storm

This home is on stilts. After a monsoon, water and mud flow under the house.

In a sandstorm this tent keeps sand out. An underground storm cellar keeps people safe during a tornado.

Wild Animals, Wild Weather

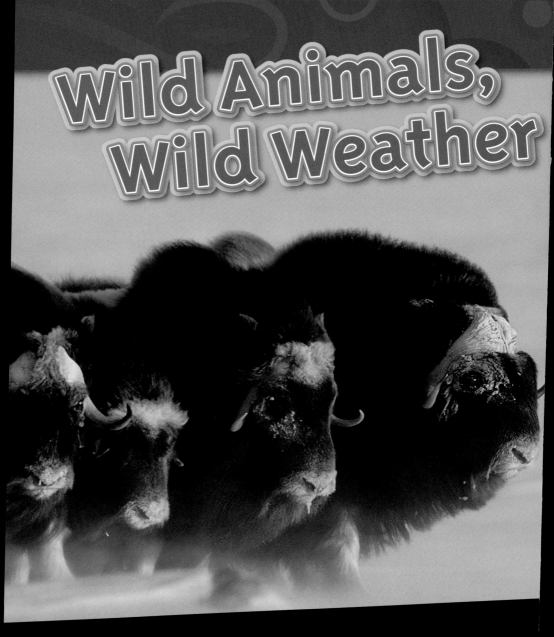

In blizzard winds these muskoxen huddle together. They face the wind so their bodies stay warmer.

In a haboob, camels shut a second pair of eyelids to protect their eyes from sand. Their long, thin nostrils and extra hairy ears keep sand out.

In monsoon rains, some monkeys keep dry in buildings or under branches. Other monkeys don't mind getting wet.

WEATHER
What it is like outside.

CRYSTAL
A shape that is the same on many sides.

ELECTRICITY
Energy that can be natural or man-made.

FUNNEL
A cone shape, wider at the top.

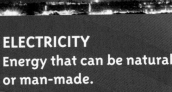

Weather

Kristin Baird Rattini

NATIONAL
GEOGRAPHIC

Washington, D.C.

To Tom and Emily, the sunshine of my life —K. B. R.

The publisher and author gratefully acknowledge the expert review of this book
by Jeff Weber of the University Corporation for Atmospheric Research.

Paperback ISBN: 978-1-4263-1348-6
Library Edition ISBN: 978-1-4263-1349-3

Book design by YAY! Design

Photo credits

Cover, Ron Gravelle/National Geographic Your Shot; 1, Robert Postma/First Light/Corbis; 2, rtem/
Shutterstock; 4–5, Michael DeYoung/Corbis; 6, Flickr RF/Getty Images; 7, Dennis Hallinan/Jupiter
Images; 8–9, Jasper White/Getty Images; 10, National Geographic RF/Getty Images; 11, Sami
Sarkis/Getty Images; 12–13, SuperStock; 14, Radius Images/Getty Images; 15, amana images RF/
Getty Images; 16, Michael Durham/Minden Pictures; 18–19, Na Gen Imaging/Getty Images; 20,
SuperStock; 22–23, LOOK/Getty Images; 24 (UPLE), sittitap/Shutterstock; 24 (UPRT), HABRDA/
Shutterstock; 24 (LO), Mark Lewis/Getty Images; 25 (UP), Minerva Studio/Shutterstock; 25 (LOLE),
Galyna Andrushko/Shutterstock; 25 (LORT), Dainis Derics/Shutterstock; 26–27, Roy Morsch/
Corbis; 28, Varina Patel/iStockphoto; 29 (UP), Miro Photography/First Light/Corbis; 29 (LO),
Richard Bloom/Getty Images; 30 (LE), Ljupco Smokovski/Shutterstock; 30 (RT), Jeffrey Conley/
Getty Images; 31 (UPLE), tale/Shutterstock; 31 (UPRT), SuperStock; 31 (LOLE), irin-k/Shutterstock;
31 (LORT), Juan He/Shutterstock; 32 (UPLE), Dainis Derics/Shutterstock; 32 (UPRT), Michael Durham/
Minden Pictures; 32 (LOLE), Popovici Ioan/Shutterstock; 32 (LORT), Digital Vision/Getty Images

Table of Contents

Look Up at the Sky

The weather helps us know
what to wear, and do, and grow.

It brings rain, wind, and sun.
Let's go outside for some fun!

What Is Weather?

Peek out your window at
the sky. Is it sunny or cloudy?
Rainy or windy? You are
checking the weather!

Weather is what it's like
outside at one place, at one
time. But keep a lookout.
Weather can change fast!

The Sun

The sun warms the land. It warms the air and water, too.

The sun's heat and light help things grow. Plants and animals need sunshine to live.

9

Sunny days are fun. You can play outside! Will you go to the park? Or ride a bike? The sun can make the air outside hot. You can cool off with a swim!

Clouds

White, fluffy clouds are called cumulus (KYOOM-yuh-lus) clouds.

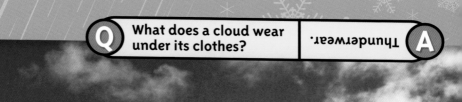

Q What does a cloud wear under its clothes?

A Thunderwear.

Tiny water droplets float in the air. They group together. They make clouds of all shapes and sizes.

White, fluffy clouds mean good weather.

Weather Word

DROPLET: A very small bit of liquid

13

Flat, gray clouds
bring rain.

Flat, gray clouds are called
stratus (STRA-tuhs) clouds.

Some clouds are
thin and wispy.
They can look
like curls of hair.
These clouds float
high in the sky.

Thin, wispy clouds
are called cirrus
(SIR-us) clouds.

15

What Comes From Clouds?

Drip, drop. Down comes the rain!

Water droplets in clouds sometimes fall as rain. Rain falls in warm and cool weather.

Rain helps plants and animals live. It fills rivers and ponds. Rain forms puddles on sidewalks. *Splash!*

Weather
Word

FLURRY: A light
snowfall that barely
covers the ground

Brrr! It's cold outside.
Water droplets in clouds
sometimes freeze. They can
fall as hail or snow.

If it's hail, you'll see ice. If it's snow, you might get a flurry (FLUR-ee). Often, a lot of snow means a snow day!

19

Lightning and Thunder

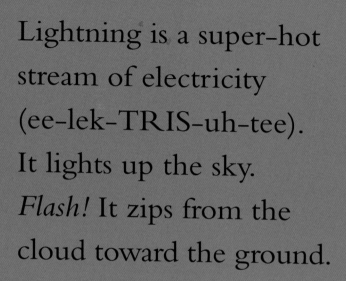

Lightning is a super-hot stream of electricity (ee-lek-TRIS-uh-tee). It lights up the sky. *Flash!* It zips from the cloud toward the ground.

After lightning comes a *BOOM!* That sound is thunder.

Weather Word

ELECTRICITY: Energy that can make heat and light

Rainbows

Have you ever seen a rainbow after a storm? Rainbows are made from sunlight and water droplets.

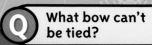
Rainbows paint bright stripes of color in the sky. Red, orange, yellow, green, blue, and purple. Which color do you like best?

6 Ways Weather Is Wild

1 Sometimes water flows where it is usually dry. This is called a flood.

2 Hail is ice that rains from the sky. It can be small. Or it can be bigger than a baseball!

3 A hurricane brings heavy rain and strong winds.

4

Very strong winds sometimes twist. They form a tornado.

5

It's hard to see in a blizzard!

6

Sometimes it doesn't rain for a long time. This is called a drought (drowt).

Wind

Wind is moving air. A light
wind is called a breeze. A strong
wind is called a gale.

Wind has energy. It pushes
clouds and rain across the sky.
Wind can make kites dance.

Weather and Me

The weather helps you plan your day. Should you wear sunglasses or rain boots? Will you swim or throw snowballs?

Wherever you go, the weather is always with you.

29

What in the World?

These pictures are close-up views of weather things. Use the hints to figure out what's in each picture. Answers are on page 31.

HINT: Wear these in sunny weather.

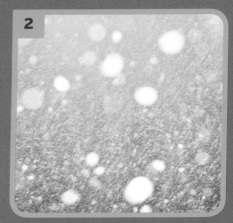

HINT: They fall as a flurry or as a blizzard.

WORD BANK

raindrops snowflakes sunglasses umbrella clouds lightning

HINT: This goes up when rain comes down.

HINT: A stream of electricity

HINT: They come in all shapes and sizes.

HINT: They fall from the clouds in warm weather.

Answers: 1. sunglasses, 2. snowflakes, 3. umbrella, 4. lightning, 5. clouds, 6. raindrops

**BLIZZARD: A heavy
snowstorm with wind**

**DROPLET: A very small
bit of liquid**

**ELECTRICITY: Energy that
can make heat and light**

**FLURRY: A light snowfall
that barely covers the
ground**

Rocks and Minerals

Kathleen Weidner Zoehfeld

NATIONAL
GEOGRAPHIC

Washington, D.C.

For my Grandad, who loved the rocks of the Catskills
—K. W. Z.

A special thanks to Steve Tomecek, a.k.a. "The Dirtmeister,"
for lending us his expertise in the creation of this book

Design by YAY! Design

Paperback ISBN: 978-1-4263-1038-6
Library edition ISBN: 978-1-4263-1039-3

Photo Credits

Cover, Dorling Kindersley/Getty Images; 1, Walter Geiersperger/Corbis; 2, Pablo Romero/Shutterstock; 4-5, Michael DeYoung/Corbis; 6-7, Allen Donilkowski/Flickr RF/Getty Images; 8, Suzi Nelson/Shutterstock; 9 (top left), Martin Novak/Shutterstock; 9 (top right), Manamana/Shutterstock; 9 (left center), Tyler Boyes/Shutterstock; 9 (right center), Biophoto Associates/Photo Researchers, Inc.; 9 (bottom left), Charles D. Winters/Photo Researchers RM/Getty Images; 9 (bottom right), Steffen Foerster Photography/Shutterstock; 10, Dorling Kindersley/Getty Images; 11 (top), Charles D. Winters/Photo Researchers RM/Getty Images; 11 (bottom), Biophoto Associates/Photo Researchers, Inc.; 12, Suzi Nelson/Shutterstock; 12-13, Tim Robinson; 14 (top), Bragin Alexey/Shutterstock; 14 (center), Visuals Unlimited/Getty Images; 14 (bottom), Glen Allison/Photodisc/Getty Images; 15, beboy/Shutterstock; 16, Jim Lopes/Shutterstock; 16 (inset), Suzi Nelson/Shutterstock; 17 (bottom), Visuals Unlimited/Getty Images; 17 (top), Gary Ombler/Dorling Kindersley/Getty Images; 18 (bottom right), Doug Martin/Photo Researchers/Getty Images; 18, Suzi Nelson/Shutterstock; 19 (top left), Michal Baranski/Shutterstock; 19 (top right), Tyler Boyes/Shutterstock; 19 (bottom left), Charles D. Winters/Photo Researchers RM/Getty Images; bottom right: 19 (bottom right), Doug Martin/Photo Researchers RM/Getty Images; 19 (bottom), A. Louis Goldman/Photo Researchers, Inc.; 20 (top left), sculpies/Shutterstock; 20 (top right), David W. Hughes/Shutterstock; 20 (bottom), Philippe Psaila/Photo Researchers, Inc.; 21 (top left), S.J. Krasemann/Peter Arnold/Getty Images; 21 (top right), Myotis/Shutterstock; 21 (bottom left), Mark A Schneider/Photo Researchers/Getty Images; 21 (bottom right), Jim Parkin/Shutterstock; 22-23, Tim Robinson; 24, Dorling Kindersley/Getty Images; 25, James L. Amos/Photo Researchers RM/Getty Images; 26 (bottom left), Mr. Lightman/Shutterstock; 27 (top left), Breck P. Kent/Animals Animals; 27 (top right), Burazin/Getty Images; 27 (bottom left), Biophoto Associates/Photo Researchers RM/Getty Images; 27 (bottom right), Don Farrall/Getty Images/SuperStock; 28, SuperStock; 29, Gary Blakeley/Shutterstock; 30 (top), beboy/Shutterstock; 30 (center), Dr. Marli Miller/Visuals Unlimited, Inc./Getty Images; 30 (bottom), Dan Shugar/Aurora Photos; 31 (top left), Cbenjasuwan/Shutterstock; 31 (top right), Bakalusha/Shutterstock; 31 (bottom left), Leene/Shutterstock; 31 (bottom right), Buquet Christophe/Shutterstock; 32 (top right), Dan Shugar/Aurora Photos; 32 (top left), Martin Novak/Shutterstock; 32 (center right), beboy/Shutterstock; 32 (center left), Bragin Alexey/Shutterstock; 32 (bottom right), Jim Lopes/Shutterstock; 32 (bottom left), LesPalenik/Shutterstock; header, HamsterMan/Shutterstock; background, sommthink/Shutterstock

Table of Contents

Rocks Are Everywhere

Walk outside and look around. You may see rocks right under your feet. Are they gray or black, tan or brown? They might be green, blue, white, pink, or even red.

Or maybe they sparkle with lots of different colors!

Pick up the rocks. Do they feel
smooth or rough? Are they heavy
to hold? Or do they feel light

Q What's a rock's favorite way to travel?

A On a rocket!

in your hands? Rocks
look and feel the way they do
because of the minerals in them.

7

Amazing Minerals

All rocks are made up of minerals. Each mineral has its own special shape, called a crystal (KRIS-tal).

Geologists (jee-OL-uh-jists) have found many minerals on Earth. Some minerals are easy to find. Others are hard to find.

Words Rock

CRYSTAL: The shape a mineral takes in a rock when the rock forms

GEOLOGIST: A scientist who studies rocks

Easy to Find

quartz

mica

feldspar

Hard to Find

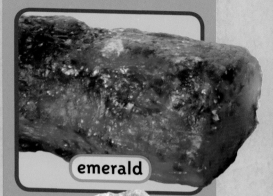
emerald

sapphire

gold

Mineral Mash-Up

Some rocks are made of just one mineral. But most rocks are made of two or more.

The mineral gold is often mixed with quartz.

Limestone is made of one mineral.

Pegmatite (PEG-muh-tite) is made of many minerals.

Rock Groups

Rocks can form in three different ways. So geologists put rocks in three groups:

1 **Igneous** (IG-nee-us)

2 **Sedimentary** (SED-uh-MEN-ter-ee)

3 **Metamorphic** (met-uh-MOR-fik)

Words Rock

IGNEOUS ROCKS: Rocks that are formed by the cooling of super hot rocks

MAGMA: Hot, melted rock that forms inside the Earth and comes out as lava

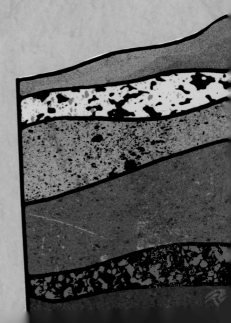

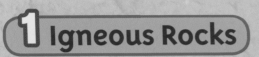
1 Igneous Rocks

Most of the rocks on our planet are igneous rocks. Igneous rocks begin to form deep inside the Earth. Here the rock is very hot. It is called magma (MAG-muh).

lava

volcano

magma

Granite (GRAN-it) forms when magma cools slowly underground.

Magma turns into igneous rock when it cools. Sometimes magma cools slowly underground.

Obsidian (ob-SID-ee-an) forms when lava cools quickly above ground.

When volcanoes erupt, magma pushes up from underground. Above ground, it cools quickly.

These basalt rocks in Ireland were formed millions of years ago by lava from a volcano.

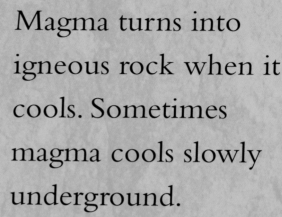

Magma that flows from a volcano is called lava.

Sandstone is made up of grains of sand.

Words Rock

SEDIMENTARY ROCKS:
Rocks that are
formed when many
small pieces of rock
are glued together

2 Sedimentary Rocks

Rocks are broken into small pieces by wind, rain, and ice. These pieces are called sediment.

Shale is made of layers of mud pressed together.

Sediment is washed or blown into lakes and oceans. The sediment sinks. It

Conglomerate (con-GLOM-ur-it) is made of many things, including sand and pebbles.

builds up in layers on the bottom.

Minerals mixed in the water glue the rock together. This is one way sedimentary rock is formed.

3 Metamorphic Rocks

On Earth we stand on huge slabs of rock called tectonic (tek–TON–ik) plates. These plates are always moving, but most of the time we can't feel them move.

When plates move past each other or crash into each other, the rocks are heated up and squeezed. This changes the rocks. They become metamorphic rocks.

Words Rock

METAMORPHIC ROCKS: Rocks that have been changed through heating and squeezing

Sandstone (sedimentary) becomes quartzite (metamorphic).

Limestone (sedimentary) becomes marble (metamorphic).

Folded metamorphic rock layers in Italy

7 Cool Rock Facts

2

Diamonds are the hardest minerals on Earth. They can even cut steel.

1

The ancient Egyptians built the pyramids with limestone thousands of years ago. They still stand today.

3

The softest mineral in the world is talc. You can crumble it with your fingers.

20

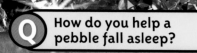

4 Some pumice rocks are so light they float on water.

5 The moon is made mostly of igneous rock.

6 A geode looks like a plain dull rock on the outside. Crack it open and there might be beautiful crystals hidden inside.

7 Obsidian feels as smooth as glass.

The Rock Cycle

Our Earth is like one giant rock factory. Old rocks are breaking into smaller and smaller pieces. New rocks are forming all the time.

On Earth, some things happen over and over again in the same order. This is called a cycle.

igneous rocks

igneous rocks

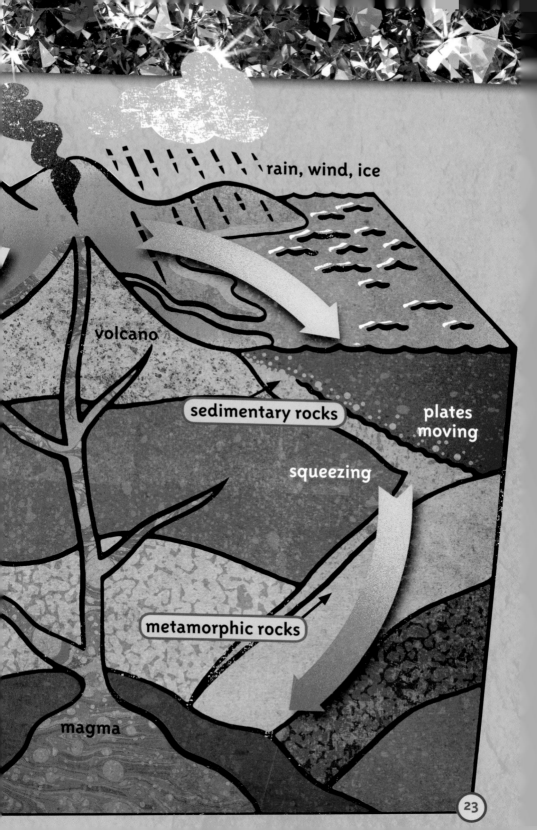

rain, wind, ice

volcano

sedimentary rocks

plates
moving

squeezing

metamorphic rocks

magma

Fossils

Sometimes shells, bones, or other parts of living things get covered in sediment. Water seeps into tiny spaces in the bones or shells.

Minerals in the water are left behind. The bones or shells turn into fossils (FOS-uls). Fossils can be found in some sedimentary rocks.

A shell fossil

A scientist at work taking dinosaur bones out of rock

Gemstones

Gemstones have beautiful crystal shapes and colors. They are often made into jewelry.

A diamond in rock can be made into a dazzling ring.

diamond

A ruby in rock is cleaned and cut. Then it is a gem!

ruby

Here to Stay

Look around you at the buildings and roads. Do you see rocks? They are everywhere!

Bricks are made of clay minerals.

Steps can be made of sandstone.

Limestone can be used to make concrete for sidewalks.

The walls of the Washington Monument are made mostly of white marble. The monument is the tallest stonework structure in the world.

Many things we build with rocks will still be standing years and years from now.

Stump Your Parents

Can your parents answer these questions about rocks? You might know more than they do!

Answers are at the bottom of page 31.

1

What comes out of a volcano?

A. pebbles
B. lava
C. sediment
D. water

2

The cycle of old rocks turning into new rocks is called _____.

A. the mineral cycle
B. the sedimentary cycle
C. the fossil cycle
D. the rock cycle

What do you call a scientist who studies rocks?

A. an astronomer
B. a biologist
C. a rock star
D. a geologist

3

In what type of rock can you sometimes find fossils?

A. igneous
B. sedimentary
C. metamorphic
D. lava

Beautiful rock crystals can be made into _____.

A. glitter
B. rock candy
C. gems
D. toys

What are rocks made of?

A. minerals
B. seeds
C. living things
D. wood

What gives a rock, like this piece of malachite, its color?

A. minerals
B. paint
C. seaweed
D. crayons

Answers: 1) B, 2) D, 3) D, 4) B, 5) C, 6) A, 7) A

31

CRYSTAL: The shape a mineral takes in a rock when the rock forms

GEOLOGIST: A scientist who studies rocks

IGNEOUS ROCKS: Rocks that are formed by the cooling of super hot rocks

MAGMA: Hot, melted rock that forms inside the Earth and comes out as lava

METAMORPHIC ROCKS: Rocks that have been changed through heating and squeezing

SEDIMENTARY ROCKS: Rocks that are formed when many small pieces of rock are glued together

Volcanoes!

Anne Schreiber

NATIONAL GEOGRAPHIC
Washington, D.C.

For Harrison
—A.S.

Published by the National Geographic Society, Washington, D.C. 20036.

Library of Congress Cataloging-in-Publication Data

Schreiber, Anne.
Volcanoes! / by Anne Schreiber.
p. cm. -- (National geographic readers series)
ISBN 978-1-4263-0285-5 (trade paper : alk. paper) -- ISBN 978-1-4263-0287-9
(library : alk. paper)
1. Volcanoes -- Juvenile literature. I. Title.
QE521.3.S34 2008
551.21--dc22
2007049743

Front Cover, 24 (top), 32 (top, right): © Digital Vision; 1: © Robert Glusic/Digital Vision/Getty Images; 2: © Shutterstock; 4-5: © Bruce Davidson/npl/Minden Pictures; 6, 32 (center, left): © Stuart Armstrong; 7, 32 (bottom, right): © Bryan Lowry/SeaPics.com; 8-9: © Yann Arthus-Bertrand/CORBIS; 9 (inset), 12-13: © Martin S. Walz; 10: © Doug Perrine/SeaPics.com; 11: © Pierre Vauthey/CORBIS SYGMA; 14 (top): © WEDA/epa/CORBIS; 14 (bottom): © Goodshoot/CORBIS; 15 (top): Mike Doukas and Julie Griswold/USGS; 15 (bottom), 32 (bottom, right): © Pete Oxford/Minden Pictures/Getty Images; 16 (inset), 27 (top): JPL/NASA; 16-17: © Phil Degginger/Mira.com/drr.net; 18-19: K. Segerstrom/USGS; 20-21: © Francesco Ruggeri/Getty Images; 22 (inset), 32 (top, left): Cyrus Read/AVO/USGS; 22-23: Gateway to Astronaut Photography of the Earth/JSC/NASA; 24 (bottom): © J.D. Griggs/CORBIS; 25 (top): © CORBIS; 25 (bottom): © Rebecca Freeman/Tulane University; 26: © John Stanmeyer/VII; 27 (center): © H. Poitrenaud/AFP/Getty Images; 27 (bottom): © Art Wolfe/The Image Bank/Getty Images; 28: © John Comforth/SeaPics.com; 29 (top): © John Harvey Photos: 29 (center): © Joseph Van Os/The Image Bank/Getty Images; 29 (bottom): © Bo Zaunders/CORBIS; 30-31: © Norbert Rosing/National Geographic Image Collection. 32 (center, right): © Jeremy Homer/CORBIS.

Table of Contents

Mountains of Fire!

Ash and steam pour out of the mountain. Hot melted rock rises up inside the mountain. Suddenly a spray of glowing hot ash shoots out. It is an eruption!

More melted rock is forced out. It spills down the side of the volcano in a burning hot river. Anything that cannot move is burned or buried.

KIMANURA VOLCANO
ZAIRE

WORD BLAST

ERUPTION: When magma reaches Earth's surface. Some eruptions are explosive.

5

Hot Rocks

When magma comes
out of the Earth it is
called lava.
The lava hardens.
Ash and rock pile up.
A volcano is born.

ASH

VENT

LAVA

MAGMA
CHAMBER

Deep beneath the Earth's surface it is hot. Hot enough to melt rock. When rock melts it becomes a thick liquid called magma. Sometimes it puddles together in a magma chamber. Sometimes it finds cracks to travel through. If magma travels through a crack to the surface, the place it comes out is called a vent.

WORD BLAST

MAGMA: Thick, liquid melted rock.
MAGMA CHAMBER: A space deep underground filled with melted rock.
VENT: Any opening in Earth's surface where volcanic materials come out.

Shaky Plates

Where do cracks and vents in the Earth come from?

The land we live on is broken into pieces called plates. The plates fit Earth like a puzzle. They are always moving a few inches a year. When plates pull apart... or smash together...watch out!

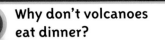

This picture shows the gap that forms when plates pull apart.

THINGVELLIR, ICELAND

Mid-Atlantic Ridge

One place where Earth's plates smash together is called the Mid-Atlantic Ridge. It is the longest mountain range on Earth and most of it is underwater.

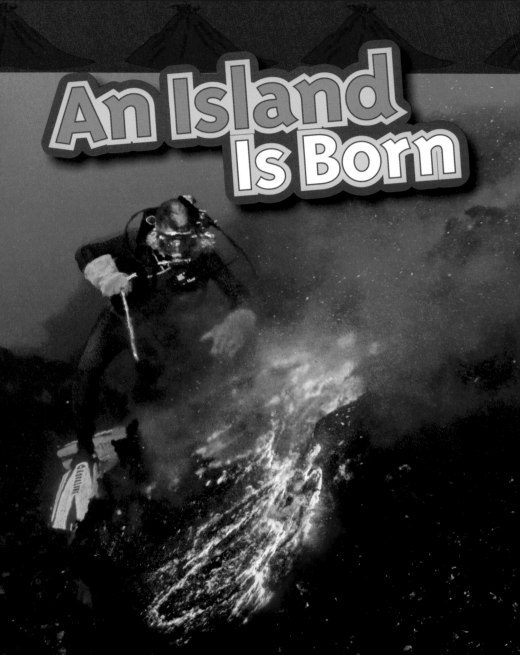

An Island Is Born

What happens when two plates pull apart?
They make a giant crack in the Earth.
Magma can rise up through these cracks.
This even happens underwater.

About 60 million years ago an underwater volcano poured out so much lava, it made new land. A huge island grew, right in the middle of the ocean. Lava formed the country of Iceland!

SURTSEY

About 50 years ago, people saw smoke coming out of the ocean near Iceland. A new island was being born right before their eyes! They called it Surtsey, after the Norse god of fire.

The Ring of Fire

Karymsky Volcano

ASIA

Pacific Oc

Indian Ocean

Mount Merapi

AUSTRALIA

Ring of Fire
Earth's plates
Mountains
Active volcanoes

What happens when plates bump into each other? Maybe a mountain will be pushed a little higher. Maybe a volcano will erupt. There may be an earthquake, or a tsunami, or both!

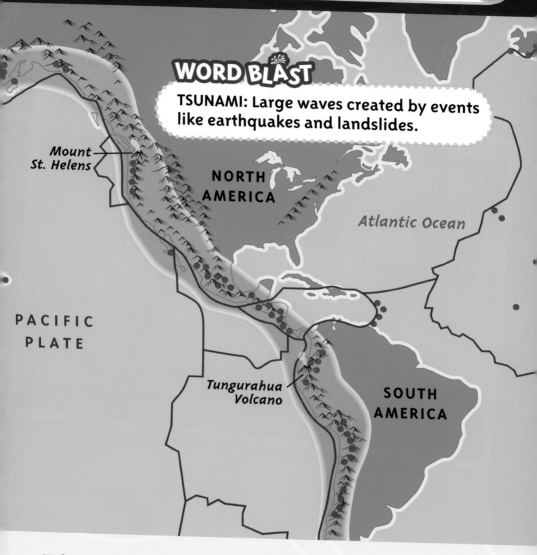

WORD BLAST

TSUNAMI: Large waves created by events like earthquakes and landslides.

Mount St. Helens

NORTH AMERICA

Atlantic Ocean

PACIFIC PLATE

Tungurahua Volcano

SOUTH AMERICA

The edge of the Pacific plate is grinding into the plates around it. The area is called the Ring of Fire. Many of Earth's earthquakes and volcanoes happen in the Ring of Fire.

Postcards from the Ring

I Lava You!

Mount Merapi, Indonesia

Moose You Very Much!

Karymsky Volcano, Kamchatka

Washing You A Great Day!

From the Cascade Mountains in Washington State

Mount St. Helens

HAVING A HOT TIME IN THE ANDES!

Tungurahua Volcano, Ecuador

Meet a Volcano... Or Three

Not all volcanoes are the same. What kind they are depends on how they erupt.

The lava from a shield volcano is hot and liquid. Rivers of lava flow from the volcano's vents. These lava flows create a gently sloping volcano.

HOT FACT

Olympus Mons on Mars is a shield volcano. It is the largest volcano in our solar system! Seen from above, it is round, like a shield.

MAUNA LOA

The Hawaiian myth of Pele tells the story of how Pele, goddess of earth and fire, built a home on Mauna Loa. Violent volcanic eruptions are said to be Pele losing her temper.

Meet Mauna Loa!

PARICUTIN VOLCANO

A cone volcano has straight sides and tall, steep slopes. These volcanoes have beautiful eruptions. Hot ash and rocks shoot high into the air. Lava flows from the cone.

One day a cone volcano started erupting in a field in Mexico. It erupted for nine years. When it stopped it was almost as high as the Empire State Building.

Even though Paricutin stopped exploding in 1952, the ground around it is still hot! Scientists guess that Paricutin spit out 10 trillion pounds of ash and rock.

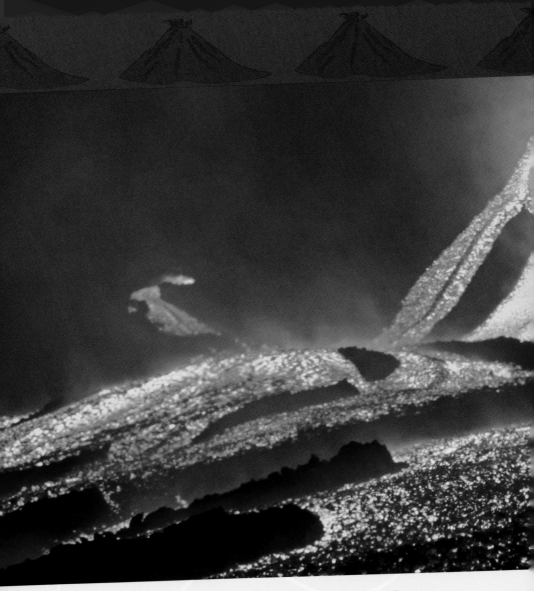

A stratovolcano is like a layer cake.
First, lava shoots out and coats the
mountain. Then come rock and ash.
Then, more lava. The mountain builds
up with layers of lava, rock, and ash.

Meet Mount Etna!

MOUNT ETNA, ITALY

There is a myth about Vulcan, a Roman god of fire and iron. He lived under Vulcan Island, near Mount Etna. Every time Vulcan pounded his hammer, a volcano erupted. The word *volcano* comes from the name Vulcan.

The True Story of Crater Lake

Crater Lake may seem like a regular lake, but it is actually a stratovolcano. It was once a mountain called Mount Mazama. Now it is a deep, clear lake in Oregon.

An explosion over 6,000 years ago blew the top off Mount Mazama. Lava, dust, and ash swept down the mountain. The mountaintop fell in and a giant caldera was formed. Over time the caldera, a crater, filled with water. It is the deepest lake in the United States.

WORD BLAST

CALDERA: A caldera is formed when the top of a volcano caves in.

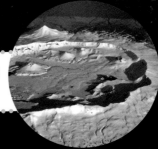

CRATER LAKE

After the mountain collapsed, there were more eruptions.
In one, a small cinder cone of ash and lava was formed. This
cinder cone pokes out of the lake. It is called Wizard Island.

Volcanoes Rock!

PAHOEHOE

 NAME: Pahoehoe (say Pa-hoy-hoy)

 HOW IT FORMS: Fast, hot, liquid lava hardens into smooth rope-like rock.

 SPECIAL POWER: It hardens into beautiful and weird shapes known as Lava Sculptures.

AA

 **NAME:** Aa (say Ah-ah)

HOW IT FORMS: The crust on top of Aa lava hardens into sharp mounds of rocks.

 SPECIAL POWER: It can cut right through the bottom of your shoes!

PELE'S HAIR

NAME: Pele's Hair (say Pel-lay)

HOW IT FORMS: Lava fountains throw lava into the air where small bits stretch out and form glass threads.

SPECIAL POWER: These strands of volcanic glass are super thin and long, just like hair! Small tear-shaped pieces of glass, called Pele's tears, sometimes form at the end of Pele's Hair.

PUMICE

NAME: Pumice (say Puh-miss)

HOW IT FORMS: In a big explosion, molten rock can get filled with gas from the volcano. When the lava hardens the gas is trapped inside.

SPECIAL POWER: The gas makes the rock so light, it can float on water.

25

Volcanic Record Breakers

Indonesia, a string of islands in the Ring of Fire, has **more erupting volcanoes** than anywhere else on Earth.

JAVA ISLAND

Q What did the astronomer say about the volcanoes on Io?

A "They're out of this world!"

The place with the **most volcanic activity** is not on Earth. It is on Io, one of Jupiter's moons!

The 1883 explosion of Krakatau was the **loudest sound** in recorded time. People heard the explosion over 2,500 miles away. Anak Krakatau, which means "Child of Krakatau," is a volcano that was born in 1927 where Krakatau used to be.

Mount Etna is the **largest active volcano** in Europe.

Hot Spots

Do you want to visit somewhere really hot? Check out these hot spots—places on Earth where magma finds its way through the Earth's crust. Hot spots are heated by volcanic activity!

The Hawaiian Islands are all volcanic mountains. They start on the sea floor and poke out above the sea. Kilauea in Hawai'i is still erupting. As long as it keeps erupting the island of Hawai'i keeps growing.

On Kyushu Island, in Japan, some people use the hot springs to boil their eggs.

Take a bath with the monkeys in Japan.

In Iceland, you can swim in pools heated by volcanoes.

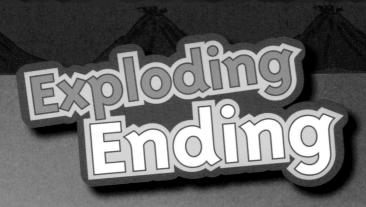

Exploding Ending

If you visit Yellowstone National Park, you will be standing on one of the biggest supervolcanoes on Earth. Yellowstone sits on an ancient caldera. Magma still bubbles and boils a few miles below ground.

Yellowstone has a lot of geysers—more than 300. The magma below Yellowstone caldera heats underground water. The water boils and bursts to the surface as geysers, spraying steam and hot water high into the air.

Go to Yellowstone and see Earth in action!

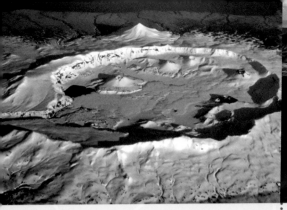

CALDERA
A caldera is formed when the top of a volcano caves in.

MAGMA
Thick, liquid melted rock.

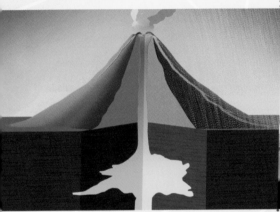

MAGMA CHAMBER
A space deep underground filled with melted rock.

TSUNAMI
Large waves created by events like earthquakes and landslides.

ERUPTION
When magma reaches Earth's surface. Some eruptions are explosive.

VENT
Any opening in Earth's surface where volcanic materials come out.